Copyright © 2019 Pauline Isaksen. All rights reserved.
No part of this book may be reproduced in any form or by any electronic or
mechanical means, including information storage and retrieval systems, without
written permission from the author, except for the use of brief quotations.

Although every precaution has been taken to verify the accuracy of the
information contained herein, the author and publisher assume no responsibility for
any errors or omissions. No liability is assumed for damages that may result from
the use of information contained within.

Dedication

To my wonderful grandchildren
Tyndale, Karl, Fredrik, Isak, Susie, Sammy and August.
You guys rock!

Acknowledgements

I wish to thank all the wonderful authors who give freely and generously of their time, talents, and wisdom to help new aspiring authors, such as myself.
My thanks especially to Dave Chesson, Joanna Penn, and Mark Dawson. They may not know me, but I feel as though I know them.

Contents

Introduction

When I say 'clueless', I mean really, really clueless. In November 2017 I decided to write a book, publish it within twelve months, and achieve Best Seller status. At that time, I had never heard of the word Indie, I didn't know what Point of View meant, and I thought KDP sounded like a radio station from the nineties. Like I said - clueless!

Less than twelve months later, on October 15th, 2018 to be exact, I released my paperback version of _Dying for Justice_ on Amazon. The ebook was released on December 26th that same year (the important reason why the ebook was released after the paperback version is explained in Chapter Nine).

On the first day of sale, the book reached the Best Seller lists for both paperback and ebook. I know because I stayed awake until three in the morning, refreshing the pages every few minutes until I hit my goal. Then I went to bed. A few days later the book reached Best Seller in four categories and soared to number one in Hot New Releases for Mystery Series. I was over the moon.

I am confident in saying that if you follow the same twelve steps I used, you can attain the same result. I really believe that. The steps are simple, not necessarily easy. There is work involved, but the steps act like a blueprint, a paint by numbers if you will, to get you to where you want to go.

I'm not trying to invent the wheel here, and to go more in-depth on certain steps I will recommend a website, book, or video where you can learn more. Most of these are free. If you are reading this as an ebook, click on the hyperlinks underlined in blue to take you to the page on the Internet. If you are reading the paperback, go to my website. www.pauline-isaksen.com, where you will find all the recommended programs, discounts and books.

I readily admit there must be other wonderful websites, books or videos where you can get just as good information. Most of the ones I recommend however, are the ones I personally used to achieve my goal of becoming a best seller.

If you're like me, you want to jump to step one and get going with the journey. But stay with me and finish this introduction. I believe it will have enormous bearing on your success and will only take a few more minutes to read. Plus, it's a very cute story.

In his book, _The Parable of the Pipeline_, Burke Hedges tells a fictitious story about two cousins living in a small village. They are given the opportunity to be paid for fetching water in buckets from a lake a mile away from the village. They love their jobs and are making more money than they ever dreamed possible. One day, one of the men considers building a pipeline from the lake to the village. While his cousin continues to carry water buckets, this young man begins investing his time and money in building a pipeline. His cousin and the villagers laugh at the young man for wasting his time and money, and for working at weekends while they are relaxing and having fun. But after many months the young man finishes the pipeline and can relax while the money 'flows' into his pockets. The moral of the story is you must invest time and money if you want a long-term successful business.

This story was important to me because I started writing a book with a business mindset. Not as a hobby or pastime, but something I would be in for the long run. That's when I began investigating the business of writing.

The following twelve steps are the result of that investigation. There are most certainly other ways and means to achieve the same result. But these worked for me and I know they can work for you.

If you're new to the craft of writing and even a tad as clueless as I was, you'll soon discover that writers have their very own terminology which they sling around at the drop of a hat. It's no surprise of course, because where you and I work we do the same thing, but it was confusing for me at the beginning. With that in mind, I've made a glossary of acronyms and explanations at the back of this book, page 38. If you come across a term that is new or foreign to you, check in the Acronyms and Explanations section to see if it is explained there.

At the end of each of the twelve steps, I give extra TIPS plus a FREE method and an INVESTMENT method of achieving that step. I use the word investment rather than cost because I believe the money used is an investment in you and your future, and not a cost that comes with no return. I will show you that you can achieve your goals with little investment; but just as a farmer would rather plow his fields with a tractor than a horse and plow, some things are worth investing in.

I've tried to use the latest up-to-date information with regard to free and investment information, as well as addresses and links to websites, etc. However, I take no responsibility for changes in these details, nor in how well or otherwise they may benefit you. Just know, I've tried to do my very best.

I've negotiated a discount for you with some of the program-owners that I recommend and have personally used. Some of these will pay me a small commission for doing so, but that is not why I've arranged the discounts. It's so you can find good programs and save money on some of the programs you consider worth investing in – something I would have loved when I first began my journey to authorship.

Tip: If you want to find more information about any of these steps, type the title of the step (e.g. write to market) into Google. By the way, a search for 'write to market' delivers 974,000,000 results in 0.46 seconds. What a wonderful age of information we live in!

Step One: Write to Market

Before you write a single word, sit down and consider the outcome.

In his amazing book, _The 7 Habits of Highly Effective People_, Steven Covey talks about the importance of beginning with the end in mind. He warns that we may work harder and harder to climb the ladder of success only to discover it's leaning against the wrong wall.

Why do you want to write? It's a very personal question isn't it? Like when someone asks, "What's your dream?" But YOU must answer that question for yourself, so you know where to place your ladder. If you want to become a best seller then don't write a book about the importance of tiddlywinks (although it's amazing to me that if you enter the word tiddlywinks into Google, you'll find over 370,000 pages dedicated to it). But to become a best seller there is just not enough interest in tiddlywinks to achieve your goal. Now, obviously, I'm exaggerating here (and my profound apologies to any of you who are tiddlywink buffs) but you get the point, right?

When I decided I wanted to write a best seller I just asked myself what people were interested in. I thought about popular television shows and came up with three things - crime/police, hospitals and legal. I also knew instinctively that the biggest market would be the U.S.A., and I know how much they love the British. So, I wrote a murder mystery about a lawyer living in London.

That wasn't very sophisticated was it? And yet, at the time, I didn't know I was doing something authors will tell you to do, called, 'write to market'.

I didn't know I would make more money by writing a series rather than a standalone. To be honest, I wasn't even sure I wanted to write more books. I had dreams of my first book selling hundreds of thousands of copies and being made into a film. But when I learned the importance of writing a series, I was glad I'd chosen a genre I could continue with.

Tip: Be careful to choose a genre you can write a few books in to begin with, you can always change the genre later if you want to.

Tip: See Chapter Eight for more information about genres and sub-genres.

Free: Discovering what you can write to market won't cost a cent.

One way is as simple as going to www.amazon.com and looking at the best seller lists. What's selling? What genres and sub-genres are most popular? What interests you and others?

Investment: Your only investment will be one of time. Your book will be easier to write if you find a genre that you are interested in and that you know something about, or that you can research. I've always been interested in crime and legal shows, but I didn't know much about either of them. So, I spent a lot of time watching these types of shows and reading these types of books. I was born in England but left there when I was twenty-six and have lived in Norway pretty much since then. So, although I have a knowledge of England, I had a lot of catching up to do. But here's the pay-off - you learn so much, and it's absolutely fascinating.

Step Two: Study the Craft

Why be a good writer when you can be a great one? If you have an interest in becoming a great writer, there is a plethora of free information online to help you become one.

When I decided to write a book, I knew I'd need a lot of help. I've been a reader all my life, but nearly everything I've read has been non-fiction. I read self-help books and business books because that was what I was most interested in at the time.

So, how was I going to write a book of fiction? Before I discovered all the help online, I did the only thing I could think of doing. I bought a bunch of paperbacks and started reading. I read about twenty books in the first month. If your jaw just dropped, let me explain something. When I say 'read', I don't mean it in the normal sense of the word. I didn't sit down with a hot chocolate and have a party. I wasn't reading for entertainment; I was reading for education. A better word would be skimming.

I skimmed the books, looking for what I needed to know about writing. Where did they put their commas? How did they write dialog? How did they show and not tell? How did they keep point of view? All of these, and many more, were new issues to me and I needed to learn them. I had a yellow marker-pen and highlighted things that I thought would help me to write my book. Then, and you will need to brace yourself for this, I tore the pages out (yes, I really did). Then I wrote on the top of the page what the highlight was about and filed the page.

I treated the whole thing as if I was going to college and used those books as if they were course textbooks. A couple of months previously (and one of the things that made me consider writing a book), I'd finished a pre-university course online. One of the courses was English Grammar and Essay Writing, and it made me realize how much I enjoyed writing, and how much I missed it. Living in a foreign land will do that to you. As I read those novels, and highlighted the information, I equated it to the online course I'd just finished and treated my writing as another course. Another thing to learn. Another thing to get better at.

As I became more used to the writing world, I started to read more information online. I was amazed at what I could learn for free. I found some great sites about writing dialog, where to place the comma, when to use a semi-colon, how to show and not tell, and so on.

Step two then, is to study the craft. You wouldn't go to your dentist for tennis lessons and you wouldn't ask your tennis instructor to pull your teeth (although he might feel like he *is* pulling teeth when he's trying to help me improve my game!). Go to the source for the information you need. To learn about writing, study a writer.

Tip: Remember the last time you had to study for something, think about the time and money you invested in it. Isn't your writing career just as important? Aren't *you* just as important? Remember the pipeline.

Tip: I was amazed to learn about a woman who has made a solid income by selling books, although she's never personally written one. She uses ghostwriters. If you think of it as a business, why not?

Free: Joanna Penn, www.thecreativepenn.com, is one of the best sites for useful information concerning everything to do with self-publishing, from writing to publishing and marketing. Joanna has a ton of free information, plus podcasts, paid books (two especially good ones here), and courses to get any clueless person off the starter block. Her book, *Successful Self-Publishing: How to Self-Publish and Market your Book in Ebook and Print* is currently free on Amazon, and I believe it's her intention to keep it so. I wish I had found her site in my early days as I know it would have saved me making some costly time and money mistakes.

Free: Dave Chesson, www.kindlepreneur.com, is another wonderful site choc-full of free information including videos, podcasts and resources for writing. Dave also has a wonderful paid product, Publisher Rocket, which I talk about in Chapter Eight when we discuss keywords and categories.

Free: www.jerichowriters.com was a particularly useful site for me to learn about dialog. This site also has more information, both paid and free.

Investment: There are many sites where you can find free information, but it's important to note that these people also have families and mouths to feed. They are running a business too, and although some information is free, other information has to be paid for. If the information is important for your business, then invest in yourself by purchasing what you need.

Investment: Here are some books I invested in to help me become a better writer:

The Emotion Thesaurus: A Writer's Guide to Character Expression by Angela Ackerman and Becca Puglish. A great book which not only helped me understand to show and not tell, but also gave me the words to use.

Characters & Viewpoint by Orson Scott Card. I bought this because I had no idea what POV (point of view) meant and I knew I'd have to understand it. A wonderful book with many elements to explain fiction writing.

Writing Fiction for Dummies by Randy Ingermanson and Peter Economy. Well hey, I was clueless right? That's pretty much the same as a dummy. I liked the simple style of this book and it led me through many of the steps I needed to learn. Its only drawback is that it ends with approaching an agent to get published and doesn't cover anything about independent, self-publishing.

Writing Fight Scenes by Rayne Hall. I knew I was going to have a fight scene in my book, so this was a good way to learn what, and what not to write.

Writing Vivid Dialogue by Rayne Hall. As mentioned earlier, writing dialog was a new element to me, and this was a short, simple to understand book.

Writing Vivid Emotions by Rayne Hall. Another great book to explain and give words to show and not tell.

Showing and Telling in Fiction and _Dialogue_ by Marcy Kennedy. Both are sub-titled, _A Busy Writer's Guide_ and again were short and helpful.

Step Three: Get Help with The Writing Process

If you could write a book and have someone look over it for grammatical issues, spelling errors, show and not tell problems and a whole host of other issues; and if they would do that for you every time you wrote a chapter or a scene or a sentence, would you do it? I know I would. And indeed, I did.

This chapter is about programs to help with writing, and no doubt there are many of them. I used four.

1. Microsoft Word is still a great composing and editing tool which I use daily.

2. www.app.grammarly.com - Grammarly is an online grammar, spell and plagiarism checking program. They have a free and a paid version. I've been using the free version ever since I started writing my book and have been very satisfied with it.

3. www.literatureandlatte.com/scrivener - Scrivener was designed by authors for authors. I used it on *Dying for Justice*, *Behind the Badge*, and *The Secret*, and I'm using it for this book (as well as my sequel to *Dying for Justice*). I confess I'm not an expert on Scrivener and I know there are tons of uses which I've not yet learned. Basically, Scrivener is a way to keep track of your book, and then make it print-ready for paperback or ebook with front matter included (title page, copyright page, dedication page, acknowledgements page). You can download a free trial program for thirty-days.

4. www.prowritingaid.com - ProWritingAid is marketed as 'your personal writing coach, a grammar guru, style editor, and writing mentor in one package'. And all I can say is - yep! It is! This is my favorite tool for writing and has the most amazing features. ProWritingAid analyzes your writing and presents its findings in over twenty different reports such as style, grammar, clichés, sentence length, and much more. I use the thesaurus constantly to find new and different words, which makes writing a lot of fun for me and hopefully, for my readers. If you decide to buy the program, you can use my link to get a 25% discount off the price, which at the time of writing is $60-70 depending on the program. You can also download a free version with nineteen reports, but you'll be limited to checking only 500

words at a time.

Tip: To learn more about using each program, search on YouTube for free instructions.

Free: Grammarly (limited functions), Scrivener (30-day trial), and ProWritingAid (limited functions).

Investment: All of the above. Try them before deciding if you want to buy them. If you buy them, you can use my discounts to save yourself some money.

Step Four: Learn about Pantsers and Planners

In the strange world of writing you are defined as either a 'pantser' or a 'planner', or perhaps even a 'plantser' which is a bit of both.

A pantser is someone who flies by the seat of their pants. They sit down and begin writing. Of course, they probably have an idea of the plot, and maybe they've done some research on the theme, but that's about it. I wrote my first book that way. I had an idea and just began writing; mainly, because I didn't know any other way.

There was something wonderful about ideas flying onto the page, and characters saying and doing things of their own free will (only a writer will understand that strange phenomenon!). I have to say it was a completely new experience to me, and one that I thoroughly enjoyed.

A planner (sometimes called a plotter) is someone who plans the plot to some detail. They know the beginning, the middle and the end, and most of the in-between bits as well. Some people love to plan, and others hate it.

Neither pantser nor planner is right nor wrong. But here are some pros and cons to consider:

Pantser:
Pros:
> 1. Allows more flexibility.
> 2. Adds to creativity.
> 3. Allows the characters to develop their own personalities.
> 4. Allows the addition or deletion of characters at whim.
> 5. Allows the writer to fill in details in later drafts.

Cons:
> 1. Can get stuck with the plot leading to writer's block.
> 2. Difficult to plan and judge the size of the individual chapters and the entire book.

Plotter:
Pros:
> 1. Knows ahead of time where the plot will go.

2. Easily gauges chapter and book length.

3. Is less likely to get writer's block.

4. Tends to write at a faster pace.

Cons:

1. Are confined to their plans which can reduce creativity.

2. May have to change the entire outline if they change something underway.

Tip: Use a recording app (or speech to text program) to record your book. This can speed up the writing process.

Free: www.jerichowriters.com (with free plotting worksheets)

Investment: *Save the Cat! Writes a Novel* - Jessica Brody (for planning).

Investment: www.udemy.com course, *Reverse Engineer Riveting Fiction & Write Best Selling Books* by Geoff Shaw. I didn't like the idea of planning until I took this course. Although I didn't use this course for my first book, I am using it for my sequel. I mention it here because it costs less than $20 and explains a great way to plan a plot.

Step Five: Call in the Professionals

Being clueless, and thus without ego (in this case) it was easy for me to want to call in the professionals. Most websites I studied recommended at least two areas that professionals were essential:

1. A professional editor.

2. A professional book cover designer.

Why a professional editor? Think back to every job you've ever had. When you started, did you know everything you needed to know? Of course not. Sure, you had manuals to read and your own previous experience, but you still needed someone to look over your work and correct any mistakes you might have made.

I was astonished at the result when I used a professional editor to look through my manuscript. Others had read my manuscript, I had already read the manuscript a gazillion times, and I had gone through a printed copy with a fine tooth-comb. And yet... my editor found spelling and grammar mistakes, plot holes and other discrepancies. Truth be told, I learned a lot from my editor.

Depending on your budget, there are three different kinds of editors in the writing business:

1. Copy editing: Copy, in the writing world, is another word for text, so copy editing is basically text editing. A copy editor will address grammar, usage and consistency errors. They're the ones who will find spelling errors and tell you where the semi-colon should go. This is the basic need of editing and is the minimum recommended for an author. After you've got your manuscript to a point of near perfection, a copy editor needs to look through it. Despite our best efforts, we all make mistakes that we don't see even if we've read the manuscript multiple times.

2. Line editing: A line editor will focus on the flow of ideas, transition elements, tone and style. They do not edit your work for errors, but rather focus on the way you use your language to communicate to your reader.

3. Developmental editing: This is the full service by editing standards. A developmental editor will help you develop your book by looking at things like plot, structure, presentation, characterization and so on.

There is nothing worse than reading a book, short story, or article that has errors - especially spelling mistakes. Poor editing will result in harsh, negative reviews - a death blow to any book.

It is generally accepted that copy editing is the minimum you should have done. I was fortunate to find an editor who did copy editing with a little of developmental editing thrown in. You can ask potential editors to test a chapter or a few pages, or to send you examples of the work they have done previously. This gives you a good idea of the kind of result you can expect.

Why a professional book cover designer? Unless you are a graphic designer, it is generally not recommended to make your own cover. Creating an eye-catching book cover that performs well often takes a major investment of time, energy, effort and skill. Good cover designers know the market and the type of style for your genre.

However, there are amazing opportunities to short-cut this process. The cover design for this book you are now reading was made for (almost) nothing. Let me explain. I joined a site, www.theauthoracademy.com which allows the member to edit a previously designed book cover. This site also includes book mock ups (commonly called 3-D images of your book), stock photos, book layouts, training, and more. At the time of writing the one-off-cost for membership is $207. When I say the design cost me almost nothing, it is because I'd already used this site for so much more and the book cover was a bonus. Of course, any future book covers I use are also included in the one-off cost which I've already paid.

Another great program, which is free, is www.canva.com. When you enter the site, under the search entitled 'What would you like to design?', write 'book cover'. A selection of book covers appear. You can further define the book cover by choosing which genre you're writing in.

To pay for someone to either edit your book, or to create a book cover, search on the Internet for help. On Dave Chesson's site - (https://kindlepreneur.com/book-editors/) he lists the different types of editors and supplies a list of editors with the approximate cost, together with the genre they edit.

The Internet is full of sites offering book cover designs. www.bookbaby.com is a professional service offering help from designing your cover to helping you design your own.

    Tip: To understand what your book cover should look like, go to Amazon and check the best sellers in your genre. For example, try 'crime thrillers', 'cozy mysteries' and 'romance' and look at the similarities within the genre, and then consider the differences between them.

    Free: Canva.
    Free: Amazon Cover Creator (available with a Kindle Direct Publishing account).

    Investment: With my first book I used www.upwork.com to find freelancers for book editing and book cover design. I ended up paying $500 for my editor, who also formatted the book for uploading to Amazon, and I paid $200 for the cover design. While Upwork freelancers are not allowed to do a sample for you for free, you can offer to pay them $5-10 to test a few pages. Or they can send you samples of their work in addition to what is available to review on their site.
    Investment: Many people recommend www.fiverr.com with the promise that you can get a book cover made for $5. I didn't find this to be true. I also found that the editors I tried (who were cheap, I admit) were terrible. But you may have better luck than I did, and I think it is worth looking at. The good thing about Fiverr is there are individual contractors who you can use for most things.

Step Six: Create a Website

There are many reasons why a writer should have a website, including the following:

1. It is expected these days (social presence).
2. It provides a professional online image.
3. It's one of the most effective ways to improve your chances of showing up in the top position if someone searches your name on Google.
4. It provides a way for your readers to find more information about you and your book.
5. It allows you to develop a mailing list.
6. It allows you to market, promote and sell your book.
7. It enables you to have a Landing Page (Chapter Eleven).
8. It's an easy way for people to reach you when you include contact information.
9. You can add a Facebook pixel helping you to customize Facebook ads (Chapter Ten).
10. It will be the first thing agents and editors look at if you decide to go the traditional route of publishing.

Making a personal website is easier today than it was five to ten years ago. Some people think they need to have certain technical or design skills to complete such a task. While that was once true, it certainly doesn't apply today. I'm fairly tech-minded, so this wasn't a problem for me. Having said that, I know for others it can be quite challenging.

I'd discovered that several writers were using WordPress to make their websites, and this is the one I also use. In fact, according to their own site, thirty-three percent of the web uses WordPress.

Some aspects of WordPress are simple enough, whilst others are more challenging. The great thing about the Internet is that if you get stuck with a problem, you can simply input a question into Google and you'll nearly always find an answer; very often in the form of a YouTube video which will show you the steps to take.

You can find comprehensive details about WordPress at: www.wordpress.org or www.wordpress.com. It is easy to get confused between wordpress.org and wordpress.com. For a clear distinction of the two see this comparison chart: www.wpbeginner.com.

WordPress is open source software which means it is free software. You can choose to have a free website, with WordPress.com controlling your website's hosting. The free version will set your domain to appear like this: www.yourwebsite.wordpress.com, and the functionality is restricted. However, they do offer a paid option to buy your own domain that can be applied to your WordPress.com website, which will then look like this https://your-chosen-name.com (mine is https://pauline-isaksen.com).

The process of setting up and running a website is outside the scope of this book, but for more information go to amazon.com and in the search box, input, 'how to make a website with wordpress'. You'll find books on the subject that are cheap, and several that are free. Here are two examples that, at the time of writing, are free:

Todd Pettee, *How to Make A Website with WordPress: No Coding or Design Skills Required*.

Brian Patrick, *How to Create A Website Using WordPress: The Beginner's Blueprint for Building a Professional Website in 3 Easy Steps*. (Plus 40+ Premium WordPress Video Tutorials).

Tip: Plugins, of which there are over 50,000 available, allow you to add additional functionality to your site, but are only available with a paid WordPress plan. Look at this site for an example of plugins available for WordPress: https://wordpress.org/plugins/. You just install them and add the functionality. Some plugins may cost money, and some may slow down your website, so don't get too trigger-happy.

Tip: When choosing your domain name, do not use the title of your book. If you choose to write more than one book, the domain name will need to be changed.

Free: I have only personally used WordPress and a simple search on YouTube will give you access to many free tutorials where people will guide you through the process. For example, at this link: https://bit.ly/2YmbmBE

Other free websites.

Free: Wix

Free: Site123

Free: SimpleSite

Free: Weebly

Free: IM Creator

Free: Webnode

Investment: Many of the above include upgrades to paid websites with increased functionality.

Step Seven: Build a Name List

I'm sorry to be the one to break the news to you, but here it is: Even if you know thousands of people, have the biggest Facebook friends list, and a hoard of Twitter followers, these are not the people who are going to buy your book. Of course, some of them will. But most of them won't. Your mother probably will, but there's no guarantee.

One of the answers is to have a big email list of fans who want to buy everything you write. That sounds nice, doesn't it? But how to grow that list? That's the problem.

These are some of the ideas I found to grow my list:

1. Many authors recommend giving away your first book for free, so that readers will buy your other books, thereby creating what is termed a read-through income. That sounds great, unless of course, you only have one book. That was my problem.

If you remember Steven Covey and the ladder against the wall, this is the time to consider which wall your ladder is leaning against. We generally *sell* a book to make money and create fans. We *give away* books to create exposure to our brand. If your goal is to make money, and you only have one book, then you must try to sell it. But if you are more of a long-term thinker and you are trying to create a fan base, then giving away your book for free, or for $0.99 is a wise investment.

To help readers find your book, you can use, for example, Facebook and Amazon ads (Chapter Ten). With Facebook, you can use a Landing Page on your website (Chapter Eleven) to collect email addresses. Amazon doesn't work the same way, but you can add a page in your ebook directing the reader to your website with the same intention.

As I only had one book, I enrolled in KU (Kindle Unlimited) Amazon's program where people can read your book for free and you get paid for the total number of pages read. At launch, I made almost as much money from KU as I did from the sale of my ebook ($0.99) and paperback ($12.99) combined. Because I didn't have another book, I offered people who signed up on my list a free copy of the forthcoming sequel (which I am in the middle of writing!). With KU's special deals I was also able to offer my book for free for five days and using Facebook ads and a landing page, I signed up more people on my list.

2. Another way to grow your list is by using 'giveaways'. This is something free that potential readers can get if they join your mailing list. I chose to give away a Kindle Paperwhite and a signed paperback copy of my book as a competition prize. The number of subscribers I got from this was just under 1,600 and the cost of the Kindle was $100.

3. Before I uploaded my book to Amazon, I offered a free copy of the book on a Facebook ad, and simply sent a pdf and mobi file to those who responded. From this, I got about 300 subscribers.

Tip: How to set up an ebook for free, permanently, on Amazon (this type of ebook is called permafree). Your ebook cannot be enrolled in KU. An enrollment in Kindle Unlimited runs for 90 days at a time, so if you are in KU, you will have to wait until the 90 days runs out before you can do the following: Upload your book to other retailers (Chapter Twelve) such as Apple iBooks, Barnes & Noble Nook, Kobo etc., with an ebook price of $0.00. Go to your page on Amazon and scroll down to Product Details. Click on 'Would you like to tell us about a lower price?' and fill in the details. Amazon will then price-match your book and re-price it to $0.00.

Tip: To set up a giveaway I used www.kingsumo.com and advertised it on my business Facebook page (Chapter Ten) and with a Facebook ad. I used a Landing Page (Chapter Eleven) with my Mailchimp account (Chapter Eleven). Of the original 1,600 subscribers I have deleted those who, after six months, had no activity on their account (i.e. they never opened a follow-up e-mail from me). This was about 50% of the subscribers. It's important to remember that offering something like a Kindle is generic and most anyone wants one. I knew that many of the subscribers would not go on to buy my books, or even download them for free when offered.

Tip: To convert a file from Word to Mobi (the Kindle extension) or pdf, I used the free program www.ebook.online-convert.com.

Free: Friends and family, especially your mother.

Investment: Advertising and giveaways.

Step Eight: Find the Best Categories and Keywords

A category, in author language, is a defined genre in which a book is written; and by which readers will find that book when they search for that category. As an example, my genre is mystery/thriller, but in that genre are many sub-genres, or categories.

When you first upload your book to Amazon (Chapter Twelve) you have the opportunity of choosing two categories. If you want to change those categories, you can do so using the link on your Amazon Bookshelf: .../Edit Ebook Details/Categories. When you do this, Amazon will delete the previous categories and replace them with the new ones of your choice - leaving you with two categories. However, if you go to the 'Contact Us' link at the bottom of the page, you can write directly to Amazon and ask them to include up to TWENTY categories - ten for your paperback and ten for your ebook.

These are the categories I have for my ebook:

1. Kindle Store/Kindle ebooks/Literature & Fiction/Literary Fiction/Mystery, Thriller & Suspense
2. Kindle Store/Kindle ebooks/Mystery, Thriller & Suspense/Thrillers/Legal
3. Kindle Store/Kindle ebooks/Mystery, Thriller & Suspense/Mystery
4. Kindle Store/Kindle ebooks/Mystery, Thriller & Suspense/Mystery/Series
5.Kindle Store/Kindle ebooks/Mystery, Thriller & Suspense/Mystery/Women Sleuths
6. Kindle Store/Kindle ebooks/Mystery, Thriller & Suspense/Crime Fiction/Murder
7. Kindle Store/Kindle ebooks/Mystery, Thriller & Suspense/Suspense
8. Kindle Store/Kindle ebooks/Literature & Fiction/Literary Fiction/British & Irish/British
9. Kindle Store/Kindle ebooks/Literature & Fiction/Women's Fiction/Mystery, Thriller & Suspense/Crime
10. Kindle Store/Kindle ebooks/Mystery, Thriller & Suspense/Mystery/International Mystery & Crime

These are the categories I have for my paperback book:

1. Books/Mystery, Thriller & Suspense/Thrillers & Suspense/Crime
2. Books/Mystery, Thriller & Suspense/Thrillers & Suspense/Suspense
3. Books/Christian Books & Bibles/Literature & Fiction/Mystery & Suspense
4. Books/Mystery, Thriller & Suspense/Thrillers & Suspense/Legal
5. Books/Literature & Fiction/Genre Fiction/City Life
6. Books/Literature & Fiction/Genre Fiction/Psychological
7. Books/Literature & Fiction/Genre Fiction/Political
8. Books/Mystery, Thriller & Suspense/Thrillers & Suspense/Crime/Murder
9. Books/Mystery, Thriller & Suspense/Mystery/Private Investigators

Keywords are words or phrases that portray your books content and reflect the words readers will use when they write into the search box in Amazon. When you upload your book to Amazon, you have free choice of seven keywords or phrases. Note that I said phrases in addition to keywords. A keyword could, for example, be the word 'thriller', whereas a phrase could be 'new thriller books'. One way to discover what people search for is to try this out yourself at Amazon.com. In the search box, click on 'All' and then 'Kindle Store' in the drop-down menu. Search for a word that matches your genre and notice all the other suggestions that appear in the new drop-down menu. These are actual search phrases made by readers.

Tip: To find the right categories and keywords was a mystery when I began the process. I studied various websites regarding this, then settled on Dave Chesson's program Publisher Rocket. This program searches all of Amazon to find the best categories and keywords for you. You can find keywords that readers type into Amazon, discover bestselling book categories in seconds, learn about other authors and their sales, find profitable Amazon ads keywords fast, and find out how many books you need to sell in one day to become an Amazon Best Seller.

Free: Search Amazon categories and keywords yourself. This is possible, but time-consuming. The way to do this is explained in this video by Dave Chesson. (**https://bit.ly/2TRqSHj**)

Investment: Publisher Rocket Cost at time of writing is $97 lifetime access. Here is a video introduction. (**https://bit.ly/2YgNLlU**)

Step Nine: Get Reviews

Getting reviews! Did you know that only one in a hundred readers ever leave a review? Some experts say it may be as little as one in five-hundred. And yet the importance of reviews for authors cannot be overstated.

Probably, each one of us has bought something online after we've read a positive review, and in the same manner, we've changed our minds about buying something after reading a negative review. When a new book is launched, readers don't expect hundreds of reviews to be already written, but they do expect some. The day I launched my ebook, I had ten reviews with an average star-rating of 4.5.

This is what I did:

1. On a site https://authormarketingclub.com/, I used a program called 'Amazon Reviewer Grabber System' to find reviewers who had reviewed similar genres to mine on Amazon. The program is easy to use and an introductory video can be found here: AMC Grab Reviewers (https://bit.ly/2CzxTSx). Begin at 2.20 minutes to see how the grabber works.

2. When you've exported the list of reviewers from AMC to Excel, you will need to send personalized emails to each of the reviewers. You can do this by sending individual emails or (as I did to get my reviews) by sending in bulk from Gmail by doing the following: Purchase the program Mail Merge for Gmail. (https://bit.ly/2YknpPW) then follow the instructions in this video. (https://bit.ly/2UVaNNe). What you are doing is taking some of the details in the exported list of reviewers, and then sending those people emails with personalized information, taken from the exported list. The details to be extracted are the FIRST NAME and the TITLE OF THE BOOK they reviewed. This is an example of a personalized, automated email.

Dear Fred,

*On Amazon, I see you reviewed the book - Ford County. I have written a similar book, and **I'm enclosing it here hoping you might do a review of it as well.** I understand you are under no obligation to review my book, and if you review it, all I ask is that you leave an honest review.*

*My name is Pauline Isaksen, and the book is a murder mystery titled, **Dying for Justice.** You can find a link to it here: Dying for Justice.*

Synopsis: When London lawyer, Julia Ainsworth, is called to defend a sixteen-year-old boy on a murder charge, she is driven to risk everything to discover the truth. But when she becomes the next target, she realizes the truth could mean justice or death - her death. In a desperate game of cat and mouse, Julia must uncover the political power-base intent on keeping the biggest secret of all.

Thank you. I look forward to your positive response.

Best wishes,

Pauline

P.S. The review needs to be left on the paperback site here, as the ebook is on pre-order until December 26th and reviews can't be added until then.

Before you send the bulk of emails, you can send a test email to yourself to see how it looks. You can also preview each email before sending, if you wish.

I sent 300 emails to reviewers which resulted in 10 reviews. Although that's a small percentage, the time to do the work was minimal.

Tip: I think it's important to send the ebook in your email (as a mobi, pdf, or doc file), rather than asking the reviewer if they are interested first and then sending it.

Tip: By putting your book on pre-order, and uploading a paperback copy, reviewers will be able to write a review before the ebook is launched. Then when the ebook goes live, the reviews from the paperback will already be on your ebook page. However, don't begin to advertise the ebook yet. With Amazon, any sales will affect your ranking immediately, but they will not count on the day of launch. It is better to wait to advertise the ebook on the day you are officially launching it.

    Tip: Put a page in your ebook at the beginning (and/or at the end) to make a call for action for the reader to leave a review. Here's the call to action I use:

ARE YOU THE ONE IN A HUNDRED?

Did you know that only one in a hundred readers ever leave a review? I'm sure more would do so if they knew how important reviews are for authors.

Please, if you can, leave your honest review at this link.

Many thanks in advance,
Pauline

    Tip: When asking for a review, include a link to the review page for your book, so people can find it easily.

    Tip: Here's an excellent video from Joanna Penn which explains different ways of getting reviews. (https://bit.ly/2OnjZYj)

    Tip: Here's an excellent video from Derek Murphy also explaining how to get reviews. (https://bit.ly/2Olzsb9)

    Tip: Good to know: From Amazon's Help and Customer Service page (https://amzn.to/2dpw6DK): 'Eligibility. To contribute to Customer features (for example Customer Reviews, Customer Answers, Idea Lists) or to follow other contributors, you must have spent at least $50 on Amazon.com using a valid credit or debit card in the past 12 months.'

    Free: Ask for reviews from people on your reader's email list.

    Free: Ask for reviews from people who've liked your business Facebook account (Chapter Ten).

    Free: Ask for reviews from people you know have already bought your book.

    Investment: Amazon do not allow authors to buy reviews per se, but it is possible to buy space for a reviewer to consider leaving a review (see video from Joanna Penn above who explains this extremely well).

    Investment: Mail Merge for Gmail - $29/Year.

    Investment: Author Marketing Club premium membership (needed to have access to the Reviewer Grabber) $97 lifetime membership.

Step Ten: Advertise

It's interesting to me that we live in a world of advertising which few of us question. We're used to seeing advertising on television, billboards, radio, magazines, newspapers and the Internet. We're not surprised by advertising, nor do we think it strange that a company advertises its products for sale. Why then, as an author, would I think differently? Because I thought by getting a book published on Amazon, people would somehow discover it, buy it, and recommend it heartily to their friends. Nope. It doesn't work like that. Even if you find a publisher, they will still expect you to do some of the work in finding readers to buy your book.

As I studied the various methods of advertising, it became clear to me that some of the most effective advertising for authors is accomplished through Facebook, Amazon and BookBub advertisements.

Let's begin with Facebook: The first time I saw the Facebook advertising page, I almost gave up the idea of advertising completely. Even being somewhat tech-minded, the site is confusing and scary the first time you see it. Today, I can go into the page and put up an advertisement in a matter of minutes. You'll be able to do the same too, so don't get overwhelmed when you first try to set up an ad.

Before you can set up an ad, you will need to set up a business Facebook page. This is a page separate from your personal Facebook page (where you are not allowed to place advertisements). Go to your home page and in the upper-right click on 'Create' and then choose 'Page' from the drop-down menu. From there, follow the set-up guidelines.

As with AMS, Facebook ads give you the ability to target your audience. My target audience is:

1. Readers of other murder/mystery authors.
2. Women aged 30-65.
3. Readers in the U.S.A and the U.K.

This means my ad is only being shown to people who fit these criteria and not, for example, those who only read fantasy. There are other ways of restricting the target group even more by, for example, saying they must also have an interest in ebooks (helpful if you only have an ebook, and not a paperback, for sale).

When I set up an advertisement, I set it to Pay Per Click, so I only pay when a person clicks on the ad. This takes them to, either a) a Landing

Page (Chapter Eleven) if I'm trying to add names to my emailing list, or b) to my book page on Amazon, where hopefully they will buy the book.

If you go to Amazon.com and search 'mastering Facebook ads' you will be directed to this page: www.Amazon.com (https://amzn.to/2OlhCoM). Here you will find several books dedicated to teaching Facebook ads at all levels. As this book is directed toward beginners, I recommend downloading a free copy of Mark Dawson's book, *Mastering Simple Facebook ads for Authors*. Not only is the book free, but Mark also offers a free three-part video series to accompany the book.

The reason I mention Mark Dawson in particular, is because when I was doing my research I enrolled in several courses. Of the first three courses I bought, I canceled and asked for my money back within the first 30-days. The fourth course was Mark Dawson's 'Ads for Authors' which I consider worth every penny and I am still enrolled today. In this course, Mark covers Facebook ads and how to use them to add people to your mailing list, sell books, monitor adds, and create an automated email sequence. There are also sections on Amazon, Twitter, YouTube and BookBub ads, and how to write good copy (blurbs). Although this is not a cheap course, the payment includes lifetime membership and all future updates to content. You can always begin by downloading the free book and video course, and then decide if you want to sign up for the full course later. Mark also does another course called, 'Self Publishing 101'.

Amazon ads (or AMS - Amazon Marketing Services) are more similar to Facebook ads than they are different. You can still target a specific audience and be charged only on Pay Per Click. The major difference is that when people are on Amazon, they are there to purchase. As opposed to Facebook where people are not necessarily in a buying mood. One restriction on Amazon is that it populates the image from your Amazon book site, whereas with Facebook, you can (almost) load up any image you have access to.

But the biggest difference is the need to input keywords into your Amazon ad. There is space for an incredible 1,000 keywords, and most sources say you should have at least 300 to be effective. This can be overwhelming, to say the least. I used Dave Chesson's Publisher Rocket , where you can find keywords that people type into Amazon when they're looking for a book like yours. Publisher Rocket will help you find profitable keywords for your AMS campaign, and once you have your list compiled in Publisher Rocket you simply export and upload it into AMS.

Another free book (this time about AMS) is *Learn Amazon Ads* with free courses by Mark Dawson.

BookBub is famous for its 'Featured Deal', and if you get your book chosen for one of these your career will take an enormous leap forward. However, the chances of a new author hitting this particular jackpot is low. You can still advertise on BookBub with small advertisements similar in content and form to Facebook and AMS. You create a Partner Page (Author Page) and go to Ads on the menu to create your ad.

Tip: To make professional-looking advertisements, use Book Brush to change your book cover into a 3-D image, and add text and background. There is a 10% discount for the Plus Plan available on my website.

Tip: If you buy a course, make sure it has a 30-day refund guarantee. Then you can see what you are buying and make a qualified decision about your choice.

Tip: If you add a Facebook pixel (https://bit.ly/2uqBqOk) to your website, you can target those people that have logged onto your website and make a targeted look-a-like audience as well (https://bit.ly/2F656n6).

Free: Mark Dawson's books and courses as described above.

Free: Book Brush (limited version).

Free: Dave Chesson: free five-part video course about AMS which I recommend.

Investment: Mark Dawson's courses. Price at time of writing, around $497-749 with an option to pay monthly installments.

Investment: Book Brush Plus Plan – 10% discount coupon code on my website.

Step Eleven: Automate Your Emails

Mailchimp is a marketing automation platform that helps you share email and ad campaigns with clients, customers, and other interested parties. Our approach to marketing focuses on healthy list management practices, beautifully designed campaigns, and powerful data analysis.: quoted from Mailchimp's page, Getting Started with Mailchimp. (https://bit.ly/2LrXhQz)

Here's the most amazing thing! Mailchimp is free up to your first 2,000 subscribers.

When I first advertised on Facebook to give away copies of my soon-to-be-published book, I quickly discovered it would be time-consuming to do everything by hand. Mailchimp has allowed me to increase my emailing list, converse with my readers, and answer them on an automated sequence.

I learned Mailchimp by using it and fiddling my way through, but for the sake of this book, I found a great video for free called 'Learn Mailchimp Fast in 35 Minutes' (https://bit.ly/2wL9PKD) and it's excellent. The author, Dorothy Shelton, also has an extended one-hour version called, 'How to use Mailchimp From Start to Finish' (https://bit.ly/2GRNSyw).

One huge benefit of a Mailchimp account is being able to make a Landing Page to grow your email list. A Landing Page is basically a website page.

Let's say, for example, you make an ad on Facebook where you are giving away a free copy of your book. When the person clicks on the Facebook link, they come to your Landing Page. Your Landing Page has a picture of the book, a comment saying free book, and text that says, 'Where do you want me to send your free book?' with an address sign-up block. When they fill in their email address they will be taken to a page where they can download your book and their name will be added to a name list of your choice in your Mailchimp program. All of this can be automated. Dorothy also has a video about Landing Pages, which is just as excellent as the other videos I mentioned. It's called, 'How to Make a Beautiful Landing Page in Mailchimp' (https://bit.ly/2OjKBt2).

Mailchimp is surprisingly intuitive (it knows what to do next) and has incredible reports. These reports will let you know how your campaign is doing, how many people are opening your email, and who is active on your email list, and much more. There are many videos on YouTube about every aspect of Mailchimp and I recommend getting to know this program.

Tip: With a Landing Page, make it as simple as possible and have only one link - the link to your free/paid book. You don't want your potential customer to be clicking on other links and disappearing from your page.

Tip: With the Landing Page or elsewhere with advertising, ask only for their email address. If you ask for more than that, (their first name, for example) you reduce the chances of them giving you any information at all. Less is better.

Tip: When listening to videos, change the speed from normal to 1.25 or 1.50. I nearly always listen to videos at 1.50, which shortens the amount of time I have to spend listening. I also watch videos when I'm exercising on my indoor bike!

Tip: Another marketing automation program many authors use, but which I have no personal experience with, is www.aweber.com.

Free: Videos by Dorothy Shelton as described above, and many other YouTube video tutorials.

Free: Books on Amazon here. (https://amzn.to/2TUqKH5) Sort by Price – 'Low to High' for the free books.

Investment: After the first 2,000 subscribers you will have to pay for Mailchimp on a gradual growing scale. Prices for Mailchimp here. (www.mailchimp.com/pricing/)

Step Twelve: Launch and Lift off!

Well done! Congratulations! Whoohoo! You now have in your hands all the information you need to write and market a bestselling book. But where will you sell it? KDP Select or Wide?

KDP Select gives exclusive rights for Amazon to be the only platform on which you can sell your ebook for 90-days at a time (you can continue to sell your paperback anywhere you like). After 90-days you can continue with KDP Select for another 90-days or opt out of it. You can opt back in at any time, but then you are committed for a new round of 90 days.

During your time in KDP Select you may not sell your ebook on any other digital bookstore, not even from your own website. In return your ebook is put into KU (Kindle Unlimited). KU is a subscription-based program that allows its members access to a large selection of titles from the Kindle store (over one million). They can borrow and browse up to ten ebooks at a time, for which they pay $9.99 a month. You, as an author, are then paid for every page a member reads. The amount paid depends upon the size of the Global Fund and the number of total pages read. In February 2019, the KDP Select Global Fund was $23.5 million. I enrolled my first book in KDP Select.

I haven't been able to discover official rates of payments for pages read, but it seems to be about $0.005 per page. This means if someone reads my ebook through Kindle Unlimited, I would earn $1.20 per ebook (approx. 240 pages). This is a good deal when my ebook is priced at $0.99 to encourage sales, and my royalty would only be $0.35. Another benefit of the KDP Select program is that you can offer your ebook at discount prices, or for free for a certain number of days during the 90-day period.

Going Wide is an author term for selling your book on as many distribution outlets as possible such as Amazon, Apple, Kobo, Barnes & Noble, and others. The easiest way to do this is to upload your book to a website like www.smashwords.com (where your book will reach Smashwords, Apple Books, Barnes & Noble, Kobo, Scribd, Tolino, Overdrive, Cloud Library, Odilio, Gardners, and more). Smashwords also has access to Public Libraries. Smashwords don't charge for their services, instead they keep about 20-40% of the list price.

Another site is www.draft2digital.com which has many of the same distributors as Smashwords above. It costs nothing to use Draft2Digital. They keep about 15% of the retail price.

For a breakdown of the similarities and differences, read Dave Chesson's review here (https://bit.ly/2pCP4yo). Please note the prices seem to be outdated, but the review is still good.

Great! You've decided where to market your book. Now to upload it to Amazon (which you'll use even if you go with Smashwords or Draft2Digital).

First, you need to create an account with KDP Publishing at www.kdp.amazon.com. Then you will need to upload your book together with some other details such as categories and keywords, and your cover. Amazon gives full information on every step of this process at www.kdp.amazon.com (https://amzn.to/2oMkeQj). They also have an introductory video here: Upload and Preview Book Content (https://amzn.to/2UTWwjI).

Before trying to do all of this yourself, I recommend looking at Amazon's free tools (https://amzn.to/2oMkeQj) page with the following information:

1. Turn your completed manuscript into a formatted ebook with Kindle Create.
2. Design an eye-catching cover with Cover Creator.
3. See how your ebook will look before you publish it with Kindle Previewer.
4. See guides for formatting your manuscript and creating a cover.

Now that your book is published on Amazon.com (and other sites as mentioned above) the time is ready to get your advertising campaign going (Chapter Ten). You can set all of this up ahead of time, so that the campaign begins at a certain time. I wanted to launch my ebook on December 26th, but I was in a cabin in the Norwegian mountains with my family, where the Internet was weak. I didn't want to risk not being able to get on the Internet to start my campaign, so I set it up a few weeks ahead of time. I had all my Facebook, AMS and BookBub ads, and my Mailchimp emails, ready to go. Everything went out over a few days beginning on December 26th and ending on January 4th.

Tip: Build up as much excitement about your launch date as possible. This is definitely the time to contact your mother (and your other friends). You can post on Facebook and your other social media about the launch.

Tip: Print business cards with the name of the book and the website addresses and hand them out. I always have them with me, and as soon as someone asks me where they can buy my book, I hand them a card.

   Free: Amazon, Smashwords and Draft2Digital (as noted above, each of these sites is free to upload your book to, and each one takes a certain commission when the book is sold). Amazon takes between 30-65%.

   Investment: Cost of business cards if you use them (vistaprint.com).
   Investment: Time, time, time. Be prepared! Good luck!

   And there you have it, my twelve-steps to achieving Best Seller status. I wish you all the best with your journey toward whatever dream you've set for yourself. And my very last tip: don't listen to the naysayers from without, and those pesky ones from inside (your head). Thousands of people are writing books, publishing them, and making money. You can too. Why not? If you'll put in the effort that's necessary, get the help you need, and decide to do it, you can be the author of your very own bestselling book.

PLEASE LEAVE A REVIEW

Are you THE one in a hundred?

Did you know that only one in a hundred readers ever leave a review? I'm sure more would do so if they knew how important reviews are for authors.

Please, if you can, leave your honest review at this link.

Many thanks in advance,
Pauline Isaksen

OTHER BOOKS AND SHORT STORIES BY THE AUTHOR

Dying for Justice – a novel

When London lawyer, Julia Ainsworth, is called to defend a sixteen-year-old boy on a murder charge, she is driven to risk everything to discover the truth. But when she becomes the next target, she realizes the truth could mean justice or death.

In a desperate game of cat and mouse, Julia must uncover the political power-base intent on keeping the biggest secret of all.

Click here to buy now from

Behind the Badge – a short story

A young woman serving a mission for The Church of Jesus Christ of Latter-Day Saints, confronts a crisis of faith when she meets an old woman who seems to know her better than she knows herself. What will this woman teach her?

Click here to buy now from

The Secret – a short story

Her husband lost his life diving from 'The Monster' . Would her son follow the same fate before she could tell him the secret?

Click here to buy now from

amazon.com

GET THIS BOOK FOR FREE HERE

ABOUT THE AUTHOR

Pauline Isaksen grew up in England but moved to Norway in 1999, where she currently resides. She and her husband, Morten (who proposed after three days!), now have four children and seven grandchildren.

She enjoys time with her family, tennis, cycling, reading, writing, and photography. She also likes to sleep!

Her novel debut, _Dying for Justice_, achieved Best Seller and #1 Hot New Release (December 2018). She likes to write exciting novels and short stories, without sex and profanity.

Here, third to the left (back row), with some of her family in December 2018.

Check out my website where you can sign up to my monthly newsletter and get a FREE short story.

Acronyms and Explanations

A/B TESTING	TESTING AN AD AGAINST ITSELF WITH ONE VARIABLE
AAC	AMAZON AUTHOR CENTRAL
ACKNOWLEDGMENTS	WHO TO THANK FOR HELP WITH YOUR BOOK
ACOS	AVERAGE COST OF SALE
ACX	AUDIOBOOK CREATION EXCHANGE
ADVANCE	SUM OF MONEY PAID BY A PUBLISHER TO AN AUTHOR
AFFILIATE	PERSON WHO ASSOCIATES WITH ANOTHER
AFFILIATE INCOME	INCOME RECEIVED FROM AFFILIATE RECOMMENDATIONS
AFFILIATE LINK	LINK TO ANOTHER'S WEBSITE
AGT	AGENT
AI	ADOBE ILLUSTRATOR
AIS	ADVANCE INFORMATIONS SELL SHEET
ALGORITHM	FACTORS USED TO MATCH QUERIES WITH PRODUCTS
ALPHA READER	INDUSTRY PROFESSIONAL READER
AMAZON	E-COMMERCE COMPANY
AMS	AMAZON MARKETING SERVICE (AMAZON ADS)
ANT	ANTAGONIST
APP	APPLICATION
APPENDIX	ADDITIONAL INFORMATION ADDED TO A BOOK
ARC	ADVANCED READER COPY
ART	ADVANCED READER TEAM
ASIN	AMAZON STANDARD IDENTIFICATION NUMBER
AU	ALTERNATIVE UNIVERSE
AUDIBLE	AMAZON'S SELECTION OF AUDIOBOOKS
AUDIO RIGHTS	RIGHTS TO AN AUDIO FILE
AUTHOR PLATFORM	WHO YOU ARE OR WHO YOU CAN REACH
AUTORESPONDER	AUTOMATIC EMAIL
B&N	BARNES & NOBLE
BACK MATTER	WHAT IS WRITTEN AT THE BACK OF THE BOOK
BACKLIST	PREVIOUS BOOKS WRITTEN BY AN AUTHOR
BARCODE	MACHINE-READABLE COMPRESSED DATA
BB	BOOKBUB
BETA READER	VOLUNTARY READER
BG	BAD GUY
BLIND FOLIO	PAGE NUMBER THAT IS NOT PRINTED
BLOG	WEBSITE THAT IS TYPICALLY INFORMAL
BLURB	SHORT BOOK DESCRIPTION
BOOK DESCRIPTION	SEE BLURB
BOOK FAIR	DISPLAY OR EXHIBIT OF BOOKS
BOOK LAUNCH	DAY A BOOK BECOMES LIVE
BOOKBUB	FREE SERVICE TO FIND BOOKS
BOOKBUB ADS	ADVERTISEMENTS ON BOOKBUB
BOOKFUNNEL	DELIVERY SYSTEM
BOOKSET	MORE THAN ONE BOOK
BS	BACKSTORY
BUNDLE	SET OF BOOKS
CAC	CUSTOMER ACQUISITION COST
CANVA	DRAWING PROGRAM
CATEGORIES	GENRES AND SUB-GENRES
CHARACTER ARC	DEVELOPMENT OF A CHARACTER
CLA	COPYRIGHT LICENSING AGENCY
CONTEMP	CONTEMPORARY FICTION
CONVERSION	SALES/CLICKS=CONVERSION%
COPY EDITOR	SOMEONE WHO REVIEWS AND CORRECTS MATERIAL
COPYRIGHT	RIGHT OF OWNERSHIP
COPYRIGHT PAGE	PAGE DECLARING COPYRIGHT OWNERSHIP
CP	CRITIQUE PARTNER
CPC	COST PER CLICK
CROP MARKS	INDICATORS SHOWING WHERE TO CROP

CROSS-SELL	SELLING AN ADDITIONAL PRODUCT OR SERVICE
CS	CREATESPACE (NO LONGER AVAILABLE)
CTA	CALL TO ACTION
CTR	CLICK THROUGH RATE
DEDICATION	PEOPLE YOUR BOOK IS DEDICATED TO
DELIVERY COST	FEE CHARGES FOR DELIVERING OF PHYSICAL BOOKS
DEVELOPMENTAL EDITOR	SOMEONE WHO GIVES IN-DEPTH HELP WITH A BOOK
DISTRIBUTION	MOVEMENT OF A PRODUCT
DIY	DO IT YOURSELF
DNF	DID NOT FINISH
DPI	DOTS PER INCH
DRAFT2DIGITAL	COMPANY WHICH HELPS TO DISTRIBUTE BOOKS
DRC	DIGITAL REVIEW COPY
DRM	DIGITAL RIGHTS MANAGEMENT
EBOOK	DIGITAL BOOK
EDITING	REVIEWING AND CORRECTING A MANUSCRIPT
EDITION	SPECIFIC VERSION OF A BOOK
ELECTRONIC RIGHTS	COPYRIGHT TO AN ELECTRONIC VERSION OF A BOOK
EMBEDDING	INSERTION OF A MEDIA IMAGE/VIDEO ON A WEBSITE
ENDNOTES	EXPLANATORY NOTES FOR SPECIFIC TERMS
ENDORSEMENT	RECOMMENDATION FROM A THIRD-PARTY
ENHANCED	IMPROVED THE QUALITY OF
EPILOGUE	SECTION AT THE END OF THE BOOK
EPUB	ELECTRONIC PUBLICATION
EREADERS	AN ELECTRONIC DEVICE USED FOR READING
EXCERPT	SHORT EXTRACT
EXCLUSIVE	RESTRICTED TO ONE THING OR PERSON
FACEBOOK ADS	FACEBOOK ADVERTISEMENTS
FC	FINISHED COPY
FEED	TRANSMISSION OF DATA
FICTION	IMAGINARY LITERATURE
FMC	FEMALE MAIN CHARACTER
FONT	TYPEFACE
FORMATTING	LAYOUT AND STYLE OF TEXT
FRONT MATTER	WHAT IS WRITTEN AT THE FRONT OF THE BOOK
FTP	FILE TRANSFER PROTOCOL
GALLEY COPY	ADVANCED READER COPY
GENRE	CATEGORY OF BOOK
GHOSTWRITING	WRITING FOR ANOTHER PERSON
GIF	TYPE OF MEDIA IMAGE FILE
GIVEAWAY	FREE GIFT
GMC	GOAL, MOTIVATION, CONFLICT
GOODREADS	SITE FOR BOOK READERS AND RECOMMENDATIONS
GOOGLE ADWORDS	KEYWORDS FOR GOOGLE ADVERTISEMENTS
GR	GOODREADS
GUEST BLOGGING	WRITER OTHER THAN THE OWNER WRITES ON A BLOG
HARDBACK	BOOK WITH A HARD COVER
HC	HARDCOVER
HEA	HAPPILY EVER AFTER
HEADSHOT	PHOTOGRAPH OF A PERSONS FACE
HOOK	SHORT DESCRIPTION TO PULL IN THE READER
HTML	HYPERTEXT MARKUP LANGUAGE
HYBRID PUBLISHERS	AUTHOR FINANCIALLY ASSISTED PUBLISHING
IBOOKS	PREVIOUS NAME FOR APPLE BOOKS
IMPRESSIONS	DISPLAY OF A POST
INBOUND MARKETING	FOCUS ON ATTRACTING CUSTOMERS
INDEPENDENT AUTHOR	AUTHOR WHO SELF-PUBLISHES (INDIE)
INDEX	ALPHABETICAL LIST
INDIE	SHORTENED TERM OF THE WORD INDEPENDENT
INDIE AUTHOR	INDEPENDENT AUTHOR WHO SELF-PUBLISHES
INFO-DUMP	TOO MUCH INFORMATION SUPPLIED AT ONCE
INGRAMSPARK	DISTRIBUTOR AND WHOLESALER OF BOOKS
IP	INTELLECTUAL PROPERTY
ISBN	INTERNATIONAL STANDARD BOOK NUMBER
JPEG	TYPE OF MEDIA IMAGE FILE
KDP	KINDLE DIRECT PUBLISHING
KDP SELECT	EXCLUSIVE PROGRAM IN AMAZON
KEYPHRASES	SEVERAL WORDS SEARCHABLE BY USERS
KEYWORDS	WORDS SEARCHABLE BY USERS

KINDLE	DEVICE FOR READING EBOOKS
KOBO READER	DEVICE FOR READING EBOOKS
KU	KINDLE UNLIMITED
LAL	LOOK ALIKE AUDIENCE
LANDING PAGE	WEB PAGE
LAUNCH	MAKE A BOOK LIVE ON THE INTERNET
LEAD MAGNET	OFFER MADE IN EXCHANGE FOR EMAIL ADDRESS
LI	LOVE INTEREST
LINE EDITOR	EDITOR WHO CHECKS STYLE AND CONTENT
LIST PRICE	PRICE OF BOOK TO THE END CUSTOMER
LITERARY AGENT	ONE WHO REPRESENTS AN AUTHOR TO PUBLISHERS
LOI	LETTER OF INTRODUCTION
MAILCHIMP	MARKETING PLATFORM
MAILING LIST	EMAIL ADDRESS LIST
MARKETING	THE ACT OF PROMOTING OR SELLING SOMETHING
MC	MAIN CHARACTER
MEDIA KIT	PACKAGE OF INFORMATION TO SEND OUT
METADATA	DATA THAT GIVES INFORMATION ABOUT OTHER DATA
MG	MIDDLE GRADE
MMC	MALE MAIN CHARACTER
MOBI	EXTENSION USED FOR STORING EBOOKS
MOCK	3-D RENDITION OF A BOOK
MS	MANUSCRIPT
MSS	MANUSCRIPT
NA	NEW ADULT
NANOWRIMO	NATIONAL NOVEL WRITING MONTH
NG	NETGALLEY
NON-FICTION	FACTUAL LITERATURE
OCR	OPTICAL CHARACTER RECOGNITION
ONIX	ONLINE INFORMATION EXCHANGE
ONLINE FORUMS	INTERNET MESSAGE BOARD OR DISCUSSION
OP	OUT OF PRINT
ORGANIC	NATURAL
PAGINATION	SEQUENCE OF NUMBERS IN A BOOK
PANTSER	AUTHOR WHO DOESN'T PLOT A BOOK
PAPERBACK	PHYSICAL BOOK WITH A SOFT COVER
PB	PAPERBACK
PDA	PRODUCT DISPLAY ADDS
PDF	PORTABLE DOCUMENT FORMAT
PERMAFREE	PERMANENTLY FREE BOOK
PH	PLOT HOLE
PITCH	VERBAL OR WRITTEN OPPORTUNITY TO PROMOTE
PIXEL	ANALYTICAL TOOL PLACED ON A WEBSITE
PLOTTER	AUTHOR WHO PLANS THEIR MANUSCRIPT
PNR	PARANORMAL ROMANCE
POD	PRINT ON DEMAND
PODCAST	NARRATED AUDIO FILE ON THE INTERNET
POV	POINT OF VIEW
PPC	PAY PER CLICK
PRE-ORDERS	ORDERS MADE BEFORE A BOOK IS LIVE
PRESS RELEASE	STATEMENT ISSUED BY NEWSPAPERS
PRINT RIGHTS	RIGHT TO PRINT
PRINT RUN	NUMBER OF BOOKS PRINTED IN ONE RUN
PROLOGUE	CHAPTER AT THE BEGINNING OF A BOOK
PROOFREADER	ONE WHO CHECKS SPELLING AND GRAMMAR
PUBLICATION DATE	DATE A BOOK GOES LIVE FOR THE FIRST TIME
PUBLICIST	PUBLIC RELATIONS SPECIALIST
QUERY LETTER	FORMAL LETTER ATTACHED TO A BOOK SUBMISSION
R&R	REVISE AND RESUBMIT
RANK	STANDING OF AUTHORS BETWEEN EACH OTHER
READER MAGNET	FREE CONTENT/GIVEAWAY
RETURN ON INVESTMENT	RATIO BETWEEN NET PROFIT AND COST
REVIEWERS	PEOPLE WHO COMMENT ON BOOKS
REVIEWS	COMMENT BY A REVIEWER
RI	ROMANTIC INTEREST
ROI	RETURN ON INVESTMENT
ROYALTY	PAYMENTS WHICH CAN BE ONGOING
ROYALTY FREE IMAGE	IMAGE WHICH CAN BE FREELY USED
RRP	RECOMMENDED RETAIL PRICE

RSS FEED	DISTRIBUTION OF CONTENT TO MANY PEOPLE
RTC	REVIEW TO COME
SCRIBD	SUBSCRIPTION SERVICE
SEO	SEARCH ENGINE OPTIMIZATION
SERIES	SEQUENCE OF BOOKS WITH COMMON CHARACTERISTICS
SEVEN TOUCHES	READER NEEDS TO HEAR AD 7 TIMES BEFORE BUYING
SF/F	SCI FI/FANTASY
SKA	SPONSORED KEYWORD ADDS
SLUSH PILE	STACK OF UNSOLICITED MANUSCRIPTS
SPAM	UNSOLICITED MESSAGES SENT OVER THE INTERNET
SPINE	MIDDLE PART OF A BOOK'S COVER
SPIRAL BOUND	PAGES FASTENED TOGETHER BY A COIL
SPLIT TESTING	SEE A/B TESTING
SPOILER	INFORMATION TO RUIN A SURPRISE ELEMENT
STOCK IMAGE LIBRARY	PROFESSIONAL IMAGES
STREET TEAMS	GROUP OF READERS WHO PROMOTE A BOOK
SW	SMASHWORDS
SYNOPSIS	OUTLINE OF A BOOK
TARGET AUDIENCE	SPECIFIC DEMOGRAPHIC GROUP
TARGETING	MARKET TOWARDS A PARTICULAR GROUP
TBD	THE BOOK DEPOSITORY
TBR	TO BE READ
TEASER	SHORT DESCRIPTION TO CATCH READER'S ATTENTION
TITLE PAGE	PAGE WITH AUTHOR, TITLE, AND PUBLISHER DETAILS
TOC	TABLE OF CONTENTS
TOS	TERMS OF SERVICE
TRADE DISCOUNT	DISCOUNT FROM RETAIL PRICE
TRADITIONAL PUBLISHING	USING AN AGENT AND PUBLISHER
TRAILER	SHORT VIDEO ABOUT A BOOK
TRANSLATION RIGHTS	RIGHT TO TRANSLATE INTO DIFFERENT LANGUAGES
TRIM SIZE	DIMENSIONS OF BOOK
TWIST	UNEXPECTED TURN OF EVENTS
TYPESETTING	ARRANGING THE TYPE OR PROCESS OF TEXT
TYPOGRAPHY	STYLE AND APPEARANCE OF PRINTED MATTER
UF	URBAN FANTASY
UNIT COST	TOTAL COST FOR ONE UNIT
UPSELL	SELLING A READER AN ADDITIONAL ITEM
VANITY PUBLISHING	AUTHOR FINANCIALLY ASSISTED PUBLISHING
VLOGGING	POSTING SHORT VIDEOS ON THE INTERNET
WC	WORD COUNT
WHOLESALE DISCOUNT	AMOUNT OF RETAIL PRICE GIVEN AWAY
WIDE	USING MORE PLATFORMS THAN AMAZON ALONE
WIP	WORK IN PROGRESS
WRITING TO MARKET	TARGETING A SPECIFIC AUDIENCE
XO	CROSS OVER
YA	YOUNG ADULT

www.ingramcontent.com/pod-product-compliance
Lightning Source LLC
Chambersburg PA
CBHW061230280526
45784CB00006B/2705